National Museums Scotland

The Romans in Scotland

Frances Jarvie

with illustrations by Alan Braby and Carrie Philip

SCOTTIES SERIES EDITORS

Frances and Gordon Jarvie

Contents

Original edition published in 1994
by HMSO publications

Published from 2000 by
NMS Enterprises Limited – Publishing
a division of NMS Enterprises Limited
National Museums Scotland
Chambers Street, Edinburgh EH1 1JF

Revised and reformatted edition 2012

Text © Frances Jarvie 2012

Images (for © information see below and
p. viii of the Facts and activities section)

ISBN: 978-1-905267-51-4

British Library Cataloguing in Publication Data
A catalogue record of this book
is available from the British Library.

Book design concept by Redpath.
Cover design by Mark Blackadder.
Layout by NMS Enterprises Limited –
Publishing.
Printed and bound in the United Kingdom by
Bell & Bain Ltd, Glasgow.

CREDITS

*Thanks are due to all individuals and organisations
who supplied text, images and photographs for
this publication. Every attempt has been made to
contact copyright holders to use the material in
this publication. If any image has been inadver-
tently missed, please contact the publisher.*

COVER ILLUSTRATIONS
Background: © Section from the Processional Frieze
(including Agricola, Hadrian and Tacitus) in the
Central Hall of the Scottish National Portrait
Gallery, by William Hole; coin (National Museums
Scotland)

NATIONAL MUSEUMS SCOTLAND
(© National Museums Scotland)
    for pages 2 (soldiers at native hillfort); 3 (Birnie
    dig, map of Roman Empire); 4 (broch); 4–5
    (glass, beads); 5 (brooches; on loan from J. V. S.
    Megaw); 6 (Croy Hill legionaries); 9 (Deskford
    carnyx reconstruction); 10 (face masks, horse
    face guard); 11 (fort drawings); 12 (coins);
    13 (grain ship); 16 (coins, Brigantia, Traprain
    silver bowl); 17 (stone altar, Arthur's Oven)
FOR FURTHER CREDITS (see p. viii of Facts and
activities section)

SCOTTIE BOOKS

For a full listing of NMS Enterprises Limited –
Publishing titles and related merchandise:

www.nms.ac.uk/books

The wild frontier

Sign on as a Trooper at Trimontium. Vacancies for all ranks.

TRIMONTIUM NEEDS **YOU**

(See pages 10–11)

How do we know the Romans *ever* came to Scotland?

Two thousand years ago, Scotland was the north-west frontier of a vast Roman Empire.

The full-scale military invasion of this wild country needed very careful planning. The Romans were very good at planning. Long, straight roads were built for the advancing troops. Forts, watchtowers, camps and supplies had to be provided for the legions of soldiers.

Two awesome walls were built to contain the people who lived in Scotland at that time. Emperor Hadrian ordered a wall between the Solway Firth and the River Tyne and Emperor Antoninus built a further wall between the rivers Clyde

Soldiers arriving at a native hillfort settlement in the Lowlands of Scotland.

and Forth. From these military wonders, archaeologists can now tell us how the Roman army lived and worked at the most northerly edge of their Empire.

Yet despite these careful plans, the Roman army never conquered Scotland, as the local tribes were experts at guerrilla warfare.

Today in Scotland there is no evidence of the fine towns the Romans built in the south of England. But we do have Scotland's first written history. A Roman historian called Tacitus wrote about Agricola, the Roman general who invaded Scotland around AD 79.

Studying finds at Birnie, near Elgin, before conservation.

Digging up the past

Archaeology has given us clues from the past to let us picture how the legions lived in Scotland. Look out for your local Young Archaeologists' Club Day Out. You never know, you might be the next person to uncover a stretch of Roman road or find a Roman coin. The past is often like a jigsaw awaiting the missing pieces!

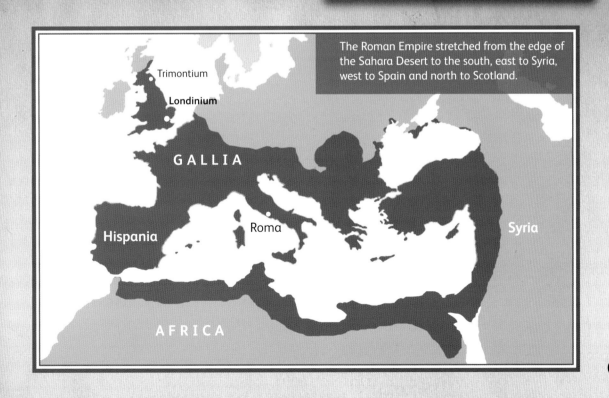

The Roman Empire stretched from the edge of the Sahara Desert to the south, east to Syria, west to Spain and north to Scotland.

Trimontium

Londinium

GALLIA

Hispania

Roma

Syria

AFRICA

Caledonia

The Romans had a name for Scotland – **'Caledonia'**. The tribes who inhabited this land were mostly people of Celtic origin.

A broch is built of drystone hollow walls. Most brochs are found in northern Scotland, in the Highlands and Islands. They had different uses. Some guarded strategic points; others were a refuge for people and their livestock.

The people spoke a number of languages, depending on their tribal origin. They were clever at making tools and weapons from bronze and iron, and jewellery from gold, silver and bronze. Known to be good farmers, they grew crops and kept cattle, pigs and sheep. They also hunted deer and wild boar for food and skins.

Men and women wore their hair long, often plaited. The men may have had long moustaches. A tunic and trousers were worn, with a cloak slung over the shoulders.

Feasting and fighting were favourite pastimes. After a battle, the people of the tribe would feast for days on end, telling stories, singing, reciting poems and drinking too much! The best warriors were rewarded with the 'hero's portion', often the thigh of a roasted boar.

The local tribes lived in homes that varied according to where they lived. To the far north were the **brochs** – tall, round, stone forts.

Brochs are only found in Scotland, and mostly on hilltops to get the best view. On hilltops they also built forts, such as **Traprain Law** to the south, in East Lothian.

Lowland tribes had wooden **roundhouses** made from timber and interwoven branches plastered with clay. But some tribes preferred houses that were built on platforms in lochs and bogs. These were called **crannogs**.

Celtic animals

Celtic tribes made brooches, such as the dragonesque pieces below, often with animal designs. Have a go at making them yourself out of modelling clay and then paint them in bright colours.

The Romans traded with some of the local tribes for foodstuffs, as they had a hungry army to feed. In exchange, the locals were given Roman pottery, glass and ornaments.

Crannogs

Visit the reconstructed crannog in Loch Tay, near Kenmore in Perthshire. Go online at the Scottish Crannog Centre: **www.crannog.co.uk/**

A crannog, or lake dwelling, was often built on an artificial island. It was made from tree trunks, layers of stone and branches.

A hidden causeway – only known to crannog dwellers – connected them to the lochside. Try the Crannog Tour and find yourself walking over water!

The Roman army

Caledonia was the main military zone for the legions in Roman Britain, and units from Germany, Belgium, France, Dalmatia and Syria all served in Britain.

Three Roman legionaries, carved in sandstone, with their shields and helmets. The carving was found in Croy Hill, Dunbartonshire, and dates to the 2nd century AD.

Latin was the language of the army, but the troops also used their own native languages. New recruits could be drawn from the people living where the unit was stationed.

There was a lot of contact between the army and the tribes of Caledonia – not much of the soldiers' time was spent

Flag standard bearer

Horn player

Signifer

Legionary

Auxiliary

actually fighting. Civil settlements grew up outside the forts – for example, at Inveresk, Cramond and Carriden.

Roman soldiers were not allowed to marry during military service, but many had children to local women or slaves and brought up their families as best they could.

Off-duty soldiers enjoyed racing, wrestling, throwing-games, hunting and fishing. They also loved gambling and playing draughts.

Order in the army was strictly enforced. If soldiers deserted or refused to obey orders, the penalty was death. Other punishments were extra duties, reduced rations or loss of pay. The Roman army was a highly organised and very successful war machine even at the farthest outpost of the Empire.

Flag standard bearer

Roman helmets were like modern-day crash helmets. They were made of bronze, padded on the inside, and with neck and ear flaps to protect the face from sword cuts.

Horn player

The **cornu** was like a French horn, used for making trumpet calls in camp and for playing tunes on the march.

Signifer – standard bearer

Each **century** or unit had its own standard, a pole made of wood, decorated with medals and wreaths awarded for bravery in battle. The **signifer** wore a bearskin (or wolf or lion) over his helmet.

Legionary

This Roman citizen signed on for 25 years and could rise to the rank of **centurion**.

Auxiliary

Enlisted from the provinces, this soldier could be made a Roman citizen after 25 years' service. Infantryman or cavalryman, he belonged to a unit of either 500 or 1000.

Centurion

Optio

The **Optio** was second in command to the **centurion**.

The **centurion** was in charge of a unit of 80 men. His helmet had a crest running from side to side. **Greaves** (shin-guards) protected his legs. His shield was made from wood in thin layers, covered with tough leather.

Trimontium Tribune

AD LXXXIV

Victory! at Mons Graupius

By Paulus Punctatim

Hill of Bennachie

Aberdee

Agricola 'not concerned'

YESTERDAY, in the Battle for Bennachie, the Roman army found itself suddenly outnumbered by Caledonians.

General Agricola said that he was not concerned, as he had a plan. Standing on the slopes of the mountain, 20 miles north-west of Aberdeen, he told reporters he intended to stretch his troop line out to the same length as the enemy.

Although enemy chariots were seen to charge at our lads, the Roman cavalry held its line and our reserve was sent around the slopes to trap the soldiers of the local tribes.

Swordsmen lend a hand

Experts in Roman swordfighting from Germany and Italy outmatched the locals with their smaller swords and larger shields.

However, in the end the battle was won by our welltrained Auxiliary forces. The legions were not called into service. But 360 of our brave soldiers were killed.

Roman soldier feels pain of battle.

Celtic Clarion

The Killing Fields

Year AD 84

By Aengus Son of Aengus

One in three brave Caledonians killed

THE Battle for Bennachie took a turn for the worse yesterday as 30,000 Caledonian forces, under the leadership of Calgacus, were placed on the hillside facing the Roman camp.

Despite placing the Caledonian chariots in front of the enemy's troops, the charge was no match for the faster Roman cavalry.

Our warriors were armed with long heavy swords and small shields, and magical protection in battle was used. But the designs on the shields gave little protection in the face of a superior force.

Charioteers were asked to drive two fast ponies at full speed through the enemy ranks and the warriors were instructed to slice off as many heads as possible. Volleys of spears and javelins were followed by hand-to-hand fighting.

Battle of Mons Graupius

Calgacus crushed

Our men were forced to retreat uphill over piles of the dead and wounded. Reserves were then ordered to attack Roman troops at the rear, but they were scattered by Agricola's cavalry. Calgacus was crushed in the chaos that followed and the tribes have been left to mourn their dead.

Facing the music

The Celtic war trumpet, known as the *carnyx*, was used during the battle to terrify the enemy. The head, below, is in the shape of a wild boar and observers reported that the scream of a pig could be heard in the way the horn was blown.

[A similar instrument, called the *didgeridoo*, found in Australia, is also known to have no holes or valves. It is reported that the sound made by the *didgeridoo* depends upon the way it is played.]

Find out more at:

www.ltscotland.org.uk/scotlandshistory/
caledonianspictsromans/

Trimontium: a Roman fort

In the 1840s, railway workers were making a cutting at Newstead in the Scottish Borders, when they came across the biggest Roman settlement in Scotland.

Below: A reconstruction of a guard for a horse's face, based on an object found during the excavations at Newstead.

Trimontium, 'the place of three peaks', was the Roman military headquarters in the south of Scotland. The fort was at the centre of the Roman road network in the country, and distances were worked out from its location.

The fort, now long gone, was built on a mound overlooking the River Tweed, in a key position. Sadly nothing of the fort can be seen today, but the Trimontium exhibition in nearby Melrose has a wonderful display of fort life and is well worth a visit.

Above: Two face masks which made up part of the parade helmets worn by Roman soldiers. These masks, and the horse's face guard (left), can be found in the National Museum of Scotland in Edinburgh.

Trimontium fort

The Trimontium fort at Newstead had a garrison of up to 2000 cavalry and infantry soldiers. There was even an amphitheatre for military parades and sporting events. One thousand craftsmen and traders made it into a boom town, making weapons, armour, pottery, glass, jewellery and tools. Many tried to make their fortune on the frontier.

TRIMONTIUM FORT

OFFICERS' HOUSES
More luxurious housing with glazed windows and underfloor heating systems.

GRANARIES
Strongly-built rooms held enough grain for a year. Ventilators let air circulate freely to keep the corn dry. Each soldier needed a third of a ton of corn per year.

PRINCIPIA
The HQ Building had offices, a shrine and pillared courtyards. The military standards of the garrison were kept safe here, as was the pay chest (kept in the strong room).

BATHS
These were always built outside the ramparts because of the risk of fire (see page 24).

DRILL HALL
Used for training men and horses. Training was hard. Men had to practise for hours, learning how to handle swords and javelins.

STABLES
Vast amounts of hay and straw were needed for keeping at least 500 horses during the winter.

EAST/MAIN GATE
To North Road, Antonine Wall, or Berwick.

WEST GATE
To farms, mines and river.

BARRACKS

BARRACKS

WORKSHOP
The army's own craftsmen provided much of the day-to-day needs of the fort. The blacksmith made tools, weapons, armour and all the iron parts needed.

SOUTH GATE
To Hadrian's Wall.

COMMANDANT'S HOUSE
The Commandant had a very important job, being in charge of troop movements. His family also stayed in the house.

Build your own fort

Build a virtual Roman fort and learn more about the Romans at:

www.nms.ac.uk/kids.aspx

Click on 'People of the past' and then 'Discover the Romans'.

An artist's representation of a Roman fort, similar to Trimontium at Newstead.

Roman ships

After the Battle of Mons Graupius, some of Agricola's ships were first to sail around Scotland, proving that Britain was an island.

It was then possible to work out the shape of Britain from the times taken to sail around the coastline.

When Agricola was ordered to advance north of the River Tay in AD 83, he used his fleet to taunt local tribes. It was easier to use ships for carrying supplies than taking them across mountains, moors and bogs.

Ships were also used to transport the vast supplies needed for the army in Scotland. Cramond on the Forth had a harbour and large stores for Agricola's troops. Careful planning went into feeding the troops.

When Roman citizens died, a coin was often placed in their mouth. This was to pay for the boatman who would ferry them to their afterlife – across the River Styx to Hades, the underworld.

As the Roman generals knew too well – a hungry army is a useless army!

Roman warships (or galleys) were long, thin and fast. They were designed for the calm waters of the Mediterranean, rather than the stormy seas around Scotland. Indeed, Julius Caesar had to go back to the drawing board to have his transport fleet redesigned after his first invasion of Britain failed.

In times of peace, warships were used for trading. Crofters in the Hebrides may have traded their woollen cloth for Roman pottery and glassware.

The Cramond lioness

In 1997 a fierce-looking sandstone lioness was uncovered by the local ferryman from the mud of the River Almond at Cramond. It was an important find, probably a memorial to a high-ranking Roman officer. It is now in the National Museum of Scotland, Edinburgh.

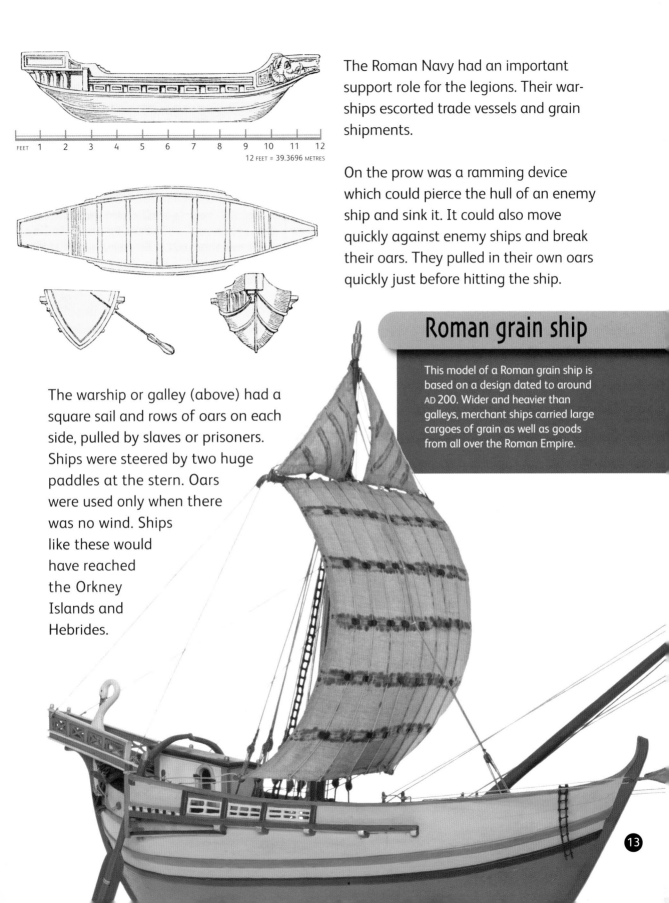

The Roman Navy had an important support role for the legions. Their war-ships escorted trade vessels and grain shipments.

On the prow was a ramming device which could pierce the hull of an enemy ship and sink it. It could also move quickly against enemy ships and break their oars. They pulled in their own oars quickly just before hitting the ship.

FEET 1 2 3 4 5 6 7 8 9 10 11 12
12 FEET = 39.3696 METRES

Roman grain ship

This model of a Roman grain ship is based on a design dated to around AD 200. Wider and heavier than galleys, merchant ships carried large cargoes of grain as well as goods from all over the Roman Empire.

The warship or galley (above) had a square sail and rows of oars on each side, pulled by slaves or prisoners. Ships were steered by two huge paddles at the stern. Oars were used only when there was no wind. Ships like these would have reached the Orkney Islands and Hebrides.

Hadrian's Wall

*'We are the scum and scrapings of the empire.
They tipped out the garbage-bin of the
Eagles to make us what we are.'*

From *Frontier Wolf*, by Rosemary Sutcliff

A posting to the boundary of Caledonia
and beyond often served as a form of
punishment for Roman soldiers. The
harsh climate, difficult terrain and
constant threats from warring native
tribes were bad enough. But years of
tough construction work also lay ahead.

The 2nd, 6th and 20th Legions were the real
craftsmen of the Wall. Twenty years later, these
same legions toiled to build the Antonine Wall
further north. This stone marks the work of the
20th Legion, 'the Valerian and Victorious'.
Note the boar, the badge of this Legion.

In AD 122 **Emperor Hadrian** (below)
visited Britain and ordered his
generals to build a wall, 73 miles
long, to stretch from the Solway
Firth to the River Tyne.

As travellers had passed on stories to Rome of the Great Wall of China, begun 200 years earlier, Hadrian perhaps decided to copy this idea. He may have wanted to impress the local tribes with the power of Rome, as well as give the army useful work to do by keeping the peaceful part of Britain safe. So it was probably planned as a boundary between the tamed tribes to the south and the wild folks in Caledonia.

The Wall was built in five-mile stretches, and there were 17 forts between each section. At every mile between the forts were smaller forts called **milecastles**. Between the milecastles were **signal turrets**.

All of these were manned by regiments of auxiliary soldiers. They came from Spain, Syria, Hungary, Germany and Africa. In 2010 the Wall was lit with flaming torches from end to end to mark 1600 years since the end of Roman rule.

Wall facts

Sons followed their fathers into guarding the Wall.

Four million tonnes of stone were used to stretch for 80 Roman miles. (See how Roman miles compare to our miles today on page 27.) It took nearly 15 years to build, and 18,000 soldiers worked on it.

The Wall became a handy source of stone for building local monasteries after the Romans had gone.

Every legion had a number of skilled soldiers known as *immunes*. Their skills as architects, surveyors, plumbers, medics, stonecutters, water engineers, blacksmiths and clerks kept them 'immune' from routine duties.

Hadrian's Wall is now a UNESCO World Heritage Site. It was so well built that large sections can still be seen today.

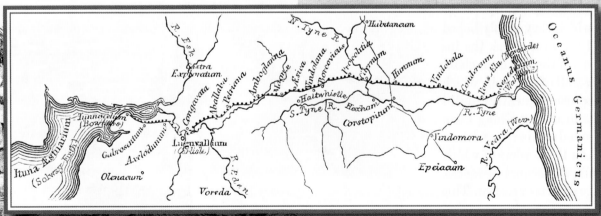

Map of the Roman Wall, between the Solway Firth and the River Tyne.

Gods and goddesses

Everything in the Roman world had a god or goddess in charge.

The gods lived everywhere – even in a flower or inside a door-latch, and most Roman coins had an image of a god or goddess on the reverse.

Romans brought their own religion with them, worshipping the traditional gods of Rome, Greece and Persia.

Mithras was from ancient Iran, and from him came the Mithraic religion which was popular in the army. Mithras was regarded as a kindly god who came between man and other gods. He is said to have killed a huge bull whose blood then gave life to all the crops. From the rest of the bull's body came all the plants of the earth. Followers of Mithras had to be brave and pass seven tests of hardship. After each test, further mysteries of the religion were then revealed.

Soldiers built small shrines outside their forts and placed statues in them. **Mars**, god of war, and **Minerva**, goddess of wisdom, were popular with soldiers. So too were the native Celtic gods.

Above: A statue of **Brigantia** from Birrens in Dumfriesshire, dated to AD 120–180. Brigantia was a local goddess, adopted by some of the Roman soldiers. The coins alongside (top to bottom) show the gods **Minerva**, **Mercury** and **Diana**.

Below: A **Nereid**, a sea nymph, one of the fifty daughters of **Nereus** (**Neptune**), features on this Roman silver bowl found at Traprain Law, East Lothian.

A temple to Victory in a circular, beehive shape was built close to the fort at Falkirk on the Antonine Wall. And the distance slabs built for the Wall often celebrated or were illustrated with Roman gods and goddesses. Soldiers also had to worship their emperor, in proof of their loyalty.

When soldiers died on active service, they were cremated. Their ashes were placed in a stone-lined box, glass jar or pot. These were then buried in a cemetery outside the fort.

During the 4th century, Christianity began to take the place of the old gods. Tombstones show that the new religion began to spread into the army. As Christianity spread through the Roman world, it eventually became the official religion.

The first monastery in Scotland was set up by Ninian around AD 400 at Whithorn, Galloway. The monks trained there, then spread Christianity in southern Scotland.

Above: A Roman soldier on guard duty stands next to a shrine embedded near a mile-post.

Right: A stone altar found at the site of the Roman fort at Castlecary, Stirling-shire. Dated to AD 140–190, it commemorated the god **Mercury**, god of trade, travel and commerce, and a favourite of Roman soldiers. Offerings would be placed in the hole at the top of the altar.

Left: The circular Roman temple at Carron, near Falkirk, known as Arthur's Oven. It was demolished in 1743.

The Antonine Wall

As a protected World Heritage Site, the Antonine Wall joined Hadrian's Wall and the German *Limes* (frontier) as part of the transnational boundary of the Roman Empire.

As the Romans extended their Empire northwards again, a new frontier beyond Hadrian's Wall was built about AD 142 on the orders of Emperor Antoninus Pius. This stretched for 37 miles, from Old Kilpatrick on the Clyde to Bridgeness on the Forth. Unlike Hadrian's Wall, which was built of stone, the Antonine Wall had only a stone base, with turf blocks and a wooden battlement on top. A broad ditch was dug on the north side, and on the south side there was a road, the Military Way, linking up the 19 forts along the Wall.

A distance slab from the Antonine Wall at Old Kilpatrick has an inscription which reads: '*To the Emperor Caesar Titus Aelius Hadrianus Antoninus Pius … father of his country, a* [detachment] *of the Twentieth Valerian Victorious Legion built 4,411 feet of the Wall.*'

You can still see sections of the Wall base in New Kilpatrick Cemetery, Bearsden. The Romans chose such a good route that the same line was taken centuries later by the Forth and Clyde Canal, as well as the Glasgow to Edinburgh railway.

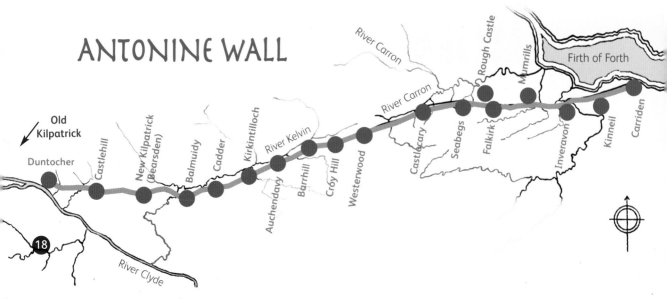

ANTONINE WALL

Old Kilpatrick
Duntocher
Castlehill
New Kilpatrick (Bearsden)
Balmuidy
Cadder
Kirkintilloch
River Kelvin
Auchendavy
Barrhill
Croy Hill
Westerwood
Castlecary
River Carron
Seabegs
Rough Castle
Falkirk
Mumrills
Inveravon
Kinneil
Carriden
River Carron
Firth of Forth
River Clyde

Most of the work of building the new Wall fell to the legions based in Britain in Antoninus's reign.

The 2nd Legion, based at Caerleon in South Wales, and the 6th and 20th based at York and Chester, all worked on the Wall. While working, the men lived in large temporary camps.

Records of their work in the form of stone distance slabs are unique – nothing similar has been found else-where in the Roman world.

When the Romans retreated from the Wall, the legionaries buried the slabs; many are still waiting to be unearthed. You can see a display of some of them at the Hunterian Museum in Glasgow.

The Bridgeness slab

The Bridgeness slab (below) was found in 1868 by a gardener. It is the largest slab to be found and it marked the eastern end of the Wall. You can see it at the National Museum of Scotland in Edinburgh.

The slab, made out of sandstone, has a commemorative inscription etched into it, recording the Roman army's dedication of the building work on the easternmost part of the Antonine Wall to the Emperor, dated to AD 142–43 (see page 28).

To the left, a Roman cavalryman aims his spear at naked tribesmen. To the right, there is an arch above legionary officers watching three animals being sacrificed at the altar. What animals do you think they are?

Answer on page 40

Left: Watch out for the **lillia** or pits at Rough Castle, Bonnybridge. They were for defensive use. Although most of the Wall has disappeared over time, the earthworks at Rough Castle, the fort at Bar Hill, Twechar, and the bath-house at Bearsden, are all impressive examples of Roman construction.

Eating, Roman style

An army is said to march on its stomach. What kept the Roman army fit and healthy?

In the army each eight-man squad organised its own cooking. Grain was stored in the fort granaries, which held supplies for a year at a time. Each unit ground its own corn ration into flour by turning two stones together. On the march, a legionary carried enough grain for about a fortnight, as well as a cooking pot, armour and weapons.

Soldiers cooked for their own unit and ate in their barrack rooms. The basics were provided by the army – corn, sour wine, meat, and oil for cooking. Food was cooked in pots and pans over open fires. Basic foodstuffs were added to by buying local produce, or using food

Bread was baked in ovens set into the back of a fort's ramparts. A fire was built in the oven to heat it, the ashes raked out and then the bread or meat cooked inside it.

parcels sent from home. Some food was brought in by road and by ship from the south.

Pork was a popular meat, but venison, small birds, chickens, milk, cheese and eggs, fish, shellfish and oysters were also eaten. Local vegetables and imported fruit added to the diet, but long Scottish

winters on duty at the Wall probably meant quite a boring diet for soldiers during the colder months.

Many plants were introduced into Caledonia for the first time by the Romans. Herbs such as mint, parsley, thyme and bayleaf were widely used in Roman cooking. It is also said that the Romans fed garlic to their soldiers so that they would fight better! In Bearsden, seeds of coriander and opium poppy have been found. These were used for flavouring. Honey was used for sweetening foods and wine.

Keeping food fresh was a constant problem. Food often went rancid and a strong sauce was used to disguise the taste. The most popular sauce was made from fish, salt water and anchovies.

Fresh meat in the winter was sometimes provided by keeping dormice (below) in small clay pots. These edible dormice were fattened up before they went into hibernation and then used as needed.

Given the variety of foodstuffs available, the troopers in Scotland were well-enough fed. Their staple diet of high-energy foods, such as bread, porridge and stews, would have alternated with more exotic foods on their feast days – just like today.

Rotary **querns** were made of two hard stones with a wooden handle and a turning piece in the centre. Querns found at Newstead were made from lava from the Rhineland. Even the Emperor Hadrian was known to grind his own corn ration when on active service.

A **mortarium** was a bowl used for grinding and mixing food.

5-a-day the healthy Roman way!

The Romans introduced new kinds of vegetables to Britain, including garlic, onions, shallots, leeks, cabbages, peas, celery, turnip, radishes and asparagus. However, if you happened to be a poor Caledonian, very few of these would have ended up in *your* broth pot.

21

Health, Roman style

Mens sana in corpore sano.
(A sound mind in a healthy body.)

Roman saying

In Roman times men could expect to live for around 60 years and woman a few years less. Those who survived into their 70s or 80s were unusual. Today, with better healthcare, most people in the developed world reach 70 or 80 and beyond.

Larger forts had their own hospitals with medical staff for the army that included doctors, bandagers and orderlies. The doctors were often Greeks, who were skilful at surgery and in the treatment of wounds.

Below: A selection of Roman medical and surgical instruments, found during the excavation of the Roman fort at Cramond, near Edinburgh. These bronze objects are dated to AD 140–210. What do you think they were used for?   Answers on page 40

Early Roman medicine was based on the use of herbs. It was a mixture of science and religion. The Romans learned a lot from the Greeks on the causes of illness, including common diseases like malaria, typhus, dysentery, tuberculosis, smallpox, anthrax, rabies and tetanus.

Fast fact

Troopers used the webs of spiders to help wounds in skin to heal.

Rod of Asclepius

Asclepius was the Roman god of medicine and healing. His symbol was a snake entwined around a staff. This is still a symbol of medical science today. But what other organisations use this symbol?

Asclepius's daughter was called **Hygeia**, goddess of health. A statue of Hygeia can be found inside an 18th-century Roman-style temple at St Bernard's Well, beside the Water of Leith, Edinburgh. Can you spot the snake?

Answers on page 40

Anaesthetics did not exist. Surgery was by trial and error. But evidence shows that the Romans were able to make artificial limbs and wealthy Romans could buy false teeth made from ivory.

Some of the plants introduced by the Romans were also grown for use as medicines. Mustard and basil were good for the stomach; lemon balm for head-aches; sage for sore throats; and for the soldiers on the Wall, hot mashed turnips were applied to chilblains!

Military medicine

The Roman army was the first to have battlefield medicine. The wounded were tended by surgeons positioned behind the standard bearer. After this immediate treatment, they were taken to the camp hospital. The standard of Roman battlefield medicine was not much bettered until the First World War. The soldier on this panel (right) is given urgent first aid in the middle of battle. The scene is part of a frieze (dated AD 106–114) on a column in Rome, Italy, erected to celebrate the military success of the Emperor Trajan.

Military doctors were exempt from guard and combat duty. They had to look after the general hygiene of the troops, as well as supervise their food and clothing.

The bath-house

Because of the very real risk of fire, Roman soldiers had to take a trip to the bath-house *outside* the ramparts of the fort.

Within the bath block was a changing room, then a number of steam rooms at various temperatures for hot and cold baths. The sweating room was like a sauna with dry heat.

Below: These well-preserved remains of a Roman bath-house and latrine or toilet area were built in the 2nd century AD. They were used by the occupants of the small fort at Bearsden, Glasgow.

After rubbing themselves down with oil, the soldiers moved through a series of rooms of increasing temperatures to open the pores of their skin. They could then remove the oil and dirt with a special scraper called a **strigil**. A dip in the cold plunge-bath then closed the pores and prevented the soldiers from catching a cold.

The warm and hot rooms in the bath-house were heated by a **hypocaust**, an underfloor central heating system. Large black stones were heated up by the furnace and kept their heat long after the fire had died down.

Hot air circulated under the floor and up the walls, providing most of the heat.

For off-duty soldiers, the bath-house was a meeting place where they could keep warm, exchange news and gamble. Even a trip to the toilet was a social event! Dirty water from the bath-house was used to flush the toilets, and instead of loo paper, sponges or lumps of moss on sticks were used.

Playing games

Roman soldiers liked gambling and made their own counters for board games from pieces of tile, pottery or shale. They also enjoyed playing marbles and dice.

Roman dice were either 6- or 12-sided. They were marked with dots or with Roman numerals.

Calculating, Roman style

Counting

Counting in tens – because of the ten fingers of our two hands – has been in use for thousands of years. Merchants throughout the Roman Empire, trading with those whose language was different, showed numbers using their fingers.

Roman numbers were made up from letters. It was easy to add and subtract Roman numerals, but much more difficult to multiply and divide. Since about AD 1500, Roman numerals have been replaced by Arabic numbers. However, you can still see Roman numerals in use on clocks and watches, on milestones, on gravestones, and in television credits at the end of a programme, often to show the date of the first broadcast.

When working with Roman numerals, remember to look at the order in which the letters are shown (see right):

For speedier calculations, some merchants used an **abacus**, not unlike a calculator today. Others used pebbles, lining them up in tens and units to speed up their adding. The Latin word **calculus** in fact means pebble.

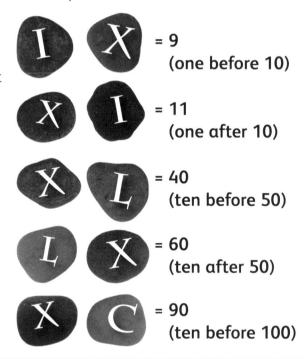

I X = 9 (one before 10)

X I = 11 (one after 10)

X L = 40 (ten before 50)

L X = 60 (ten after 50)

X C = 90 (ten before 100)

ROMAN									
I	II	III	IV	V	VI	VII	VIII	IX	X
1	2	3	4	5	6	7	8	9	10

ARABIC

Measuring

The calculation of distance was important to the Romans in their building of roads and walls. As the Latin for 1000 is **mille**, the distance a soldier could go in 1000 paces became known as a mile. A pace was in fact two strides and the Roman mile was approximately 1618 yards or 1475 metres.

The stone slabs along the Antonine Wall record the length of the Wall completed by each legion (see more about the Bridgeness slab on pages 19 and 28).

Below: A Roman using a **groma**, a tool for laying out straight lines and right angles in roads, buildings and military camps. It was simple to make, easy to carry, and known as 'the tool that built an Empire'.

ROMAN			
L	**C**	**D**	**M**
50	100	500	1000

ARABIC

First portable calculator

The abacus made Roman arithmetic only slightly easier! Roman numerals are hard to work with – especially if you multiply or divide. Engineers and surveyors, as well as merchants, used an abacus to do their work.

Abacuses have been in use over many centuries and in many countries. Compare this Chinese abacus below with an early pocket calculator, dated 1974.

Number riddles

What is the Roman number that becomes one more, when one is taken away from it?

What is the Roman number that becomes ten more, when ten is taken away from it?

And can you work out the Arabic numbers from the following Roman numerals (remember to look at the *order* of the letters):

XVI CCV XLII DCIX
MD MMX DXXX

Answers on page 40

Latin alphabet and language

The Romans may have occupied Britain for hundreds of years, but their language, Latin, never became the national language.

Below and opposite: The Romans used a **stylus** to write with, scratching words into a tablet.

Below: The Latin inscription from the Bridgeness slab (see also page 19) reads: '*For the Emperor Caesar Titus Aelius Hadrianus Antoninus Pius, Father of his Country, the second Augustan Legion completed* [the Wall] *over a distance of 4652 paces*'.

Local tribes would only have learned short Latin words that were easy to pronounce and remember, and mostly connected with trading, travel and food. When the Roman troops withdrew, locals carried on with their native language, but some Latin words remained in use.

Yet despite this, the Latin language was understood throughout the Empire and was the official language of the Church and State for centuries. Latin became an international language for science and scholarship, and plants and animals are still classified with Latin names to this day. Latin also provided terminology for law and medicine that is still in use.

So the Latin language, although no longer spoken, lives on, and our present English language has been enriched by it.

Nota bene

Many Latin words and phrases are still in use today. How many of the following do you know?

ante meridiem = before noon (you may recognise it as 'a.m.' when referring to clock times). After noon is *post meridiem* (or 'p.m.')

bona fide = in good faith, genuine

carpe diem = enjoy the present day

exempli gratia = for example (abbreviated as 'e.g.')

nota bene = note well or take note (abbreviated as 'n.b.')

tempus fugit = time flies

vice versa = the other way round

The Classical Latin alphabet had only 23 letters. It did not contain any **J**, **V** or **W** characters. Then, during the period of the Middle Ages (around AD 1500), the Roman **I** was divided up into **I** and **J**. The **V** was also, at this time, split into **U**, **V** and **W** (so 'ianuarius' became 'january' and 'iulius' became 'july').

Wooden writing tablets (below) were used by the Roman army to record orders and supplies. They wrote in ink on wooden tablets and joined them together like a concertina. The tablets then opened out in order, like unfolding a computer print-out.

Julius Caesar's secret code

The Romans were skilled at sending secret messages by code. **Caesar's Alphabet** was one particular code used by the Roman Emperor **Julius Caesar** (left). The normal alphabet was written out and underneath it the alphabet was written out again – but this time beginning with the letter **D**. This second alphabet was then used to code messages.

So if Caesar wanted to send the message **INVADE BRITAIN**, then **I** becomes **L**, and **N** becomes **Q**, and so on. The whole message would then read: **LQYDGH EULWDLQ**

Now try to decode the following secret message, sent from the front-line: **ZLQWHU HQGOHVV LQ FDOHGRQLD. VHQG PRUH VXSSOLHV.**

Answer on page 40

A B C D E F G H I J K L M N O P Q R S T U V W X Y Z
D E F G H I J K L M N O P Q R S T U V W X Y Z A B C

Roman technology

All roads lead to Rome ...

Old saying

Roads

Put simply, all the roads of the Empire spread out from Rome. Because of their superb skills in surveying and engineering, it was, at one time, possible to cross the entire Roman Empire, from Hadrian's Wall to Egypt, by highways and decent roads.

The legions planned routes and built with such care that, even after they had left Britain, their roads or routes continued in use for centuries. Nearly 500 miles of road were made in Scotland. The most important started at Corbridge on Hadrian's Wall, crossed the Cheviot Hills, then on to Edinburgh. Dere Street is the basis of much of the present A68 route.

Below, right: Remains of a wheel from Newstead. The Romans did not invent wheels with spokes, but were good at using the technology of other races.

Background: The Eildon Hills as they would have been seen while walking along Dere Street.

Opposite: Evidence for Roman technology used at the fort at Newstead and further south at Wroxeter in England, where **calthrops** were found. These four-spiked weapons were used in number to halt an enemy's advance over ground. Also featured are (clockwise from top, right) a bronze key, a Roman shoe (**calceus**) made from leather, a piece of leather, and iron javelin heads.

Tar-macadam!

Not until the early 1700s, when General Wade built a network of military roads, and John McAdam used tar for road surfaces in the early 1800s, did our roads match Roman standards.

Weapons

A soldier's weapons included a short double-edged sword (**gladius**), a dagger and two spears (**pila**). The spear (or javelin) had a jagged iron head and was designed to bend on impact. Then it could not be thrown back by the enemy!

Larger weapons were designed for use in battle or in a siege. The battering ram was the simplest. It was a heavy beam made from a complete tree trunk, set inside a wooden frame. Swung backwards and forwards, it was used to break down gates of a town or fort. The **onager** (or catapult) fired huge stones up to 60 kilograms in weight, over 200 metres distance. The **ballista** was a small field-gun which fired arrows or bolts. This lethal weapon could hit its target up to 500 metres.

CALTHROPS   JAVELIN HEADS

Metal-working

The Romans used iron locks and bronze keys. The pay-master would have needed such security to deliver the troops' wages – they were only paid once every three months!

KEY

Metal-workers also made specialist knives for tasks like shoe-making and leatherwork. (Only soldiers posted to chilly places like Caledonia were allowed to wear leather breeches.)

LEATHER ITEMS

The Post!

Soldiers at the front line wrote home when they had time off from other duties. Couriers used the road networks and good means of communication were deemed essential for the Empire to function.

A fragment of a letter, written on a thin wooden writing tablet, was found at the fort of Vindolanda on Hadrian's Wall. It said:

I HAVE SENT YOU …
PAIRS OF SOCKS
FROM SATTUA,
TWO PAIRS OF SANDALS
AND TWO PAIRS OF
UNDERPANTS.

Wooden writing tablets, such as the one on page 29, were used in large numbers by the Roman army in the administration of its duties.

Transport and trade

Traders had a busy time around the Roman forts, bartering or selling food, animals and cloth.

Trade with the rest of the Empire was also important. Luxury goods, such as wine and fruit, glass and high-quality pottery, were imported – often solely for officer use. Officers and centurions enjoyed a much higher standard of living. They preferred crockery of glossy Samian-ware made in France, together with glass and bronze vessels.

The food imported was contained in **amphorae** of different shapes according to the contents, or from which country they came. The carrot-shaped amphorae came from the Mediterranean and may have contained beans, lentils, honey, salted fish, dried fruit, cherries, plums, figs or dates.

The Falkirk Tartan

The above pot of red clay was opened to reveal a hoard of 1925 Roman silver coins. It was found at Falkirk and has been dated to about AD 230.

Inside the jar, at the mouth of the pot, there was a small piece of cloth. This woollen fragment appeared to have a simple check-woven design, similar to the more recognisable 'Shepherd's Plaid', a traditional wrap worn by shepherds tending their flocks in the worst of the weather.

The cloth fragment became known as the 'Falkirk Tartan'.

Most amphorae found in Scotland came from around Seville and Cordoba in the south of Spain. They were shipped to Marseilles in the south of France, taken by boat northwards up the River Rhone, down the River Rhine by barge, and across the Channel to Britain. And all this happened before our present-day European Union!

Food supplies to garrisons were taken in long columns of ox- or horse-drawn carts and wagons, using the great road system of the Empire. These same carts also carried gravel for surfacing roads, building stone from quarries, or military equipment – they were multi-purpose vehicles!

Large quantities of supplies were brought north to Scotland by merchant ships. Harbours at Inveresk and Cramond on the Forth, Carpow on the Tay, and Irvine on the Clyde, had roads linking up with the forts.

Many amphorae have been discovered in ancient shipwrecks.

A restored amphora from the site at Newstead, dated to AD 80–180.

The amphora unit

Roman trade and commerce relied upon the use of standard measures.

A standard amphora was kept in the Temple of Jupiter in Rome. Other amphorae could be compared to it.

This amphora was the unit used to work out the shipping weight for sea transport.

The modern-day terms 'mile', 'pound' and 'ounce' can be traced back to Roman weights and measures.

The legacy of Rome

Look again ...

A personal computer has a choice of fonts with amazing names. Some are connected to the Romans or Roman language – such as **TRAJAN PRO**, **Wide Latin**, Century Schoolbook, and the popular font **Times Roman**.

Times is used widely as it is easy to read. It was first used in *The Times* newspaper in 1932.

What is the difference between **roman** and **italic** styles of type?

Answer on page 40

In AD 410, Roman troops were officially withdrawn from Britain to defend Italy from attack.

However, through the centuries much of their way of life has survived. There are many features of daily life in Britain which came from the Romans and which are now taken for granted.

Language

Although no one speaks Latin any more, it is the root of European languages such as French, Spanish, Italian, Romanian, Portuguese and Catalan. Worldwide, nearly 700 million people speak a **Romance language**, or one based on Latin.

Scots law, based on the Roman system, uses many legal terms which come directly from Latin.

Bridges

Roman architects were excellent engineers. They were the first to use the arch for bridge building. Their designs have never been bettered and were copied by 19th-century railway engineers for their viaducts.

There are many other remnants of the Roman occupation of Britain ...

A viaduct at Leaderfoot, Roxburgh. Also known as the Drybridge Railway Viaduct, it was built for the Berwickshire Railway in 1865.

Buildings

The Romans set a great example of how to build with fine stonework. Many public buildings in Britain look like Roman temples.

The Romans were also first to use concrete. Archaeologists have found Roman mortar so hard after 2000 years that their drills can go through the surrounding rock more easily than the mortar!

We have also inherited glass windows and central heating from the Romans.

Coinage and banking

Coins were originally minted to pay the wages of soldiers and to make the collection of taxes easier.

The symbol '**£**' is used to stand for one pound of British money, from the Roman **libra** – a pound in weight. One pound sterling used to equal a pound weight in silver.

Roman numerals

Clocks, watches and sundials often have Roman numerals. Sometimes the dials show '4' as 'IIII' instead of 'IV'.

Planets

Apart from Earth, the planets in our solar system are named after Roman gods and goddesses. Can you name them? (Answers on page 40)

The calendar

The Roman year originally had only 10 months. **Septem**ber was the seventh month (**septem** means 'seven' in Latin) and **Decem**ber the tenth (**decem** means 'ten'). Julius Caesar reformed the calendar. His scientists calculated that the solar year lasted 365 and a quarter days. Every fourth year was to have an extra day added. A new month was called **Julius** or July to honour Julius Caesar. Unfortunately those in charge got it wrong: a second new month was required. It was named **Augustus** or August to honour Emperor Augustus.

Did you know?

The glint of gold ...

The Celtic people loved decoration and ornament. When the Romans entered Strathclyde, they were met by 300 Celtic chiefs wearing torcs of pure gold around their necks. These torcs were made from gold that had been collected from the upland streams that flowed into the River Clyde.

Nails vanish!

Nearly one million nails – each hand-made – were buried by the Romans at a fortress near Dunkeld on the River Tay. They had to abandon the fort and did not want the precious iron to fall into enemy hands. If the cache had been found by the locals, they would have had the nails re-made into swords and spears.

Napoleon's treasure

The stunning Warwick Vase, which can be seen in the Burrell Collection in Glasgow, was reconstructed from pieces found in a lake by Hadrian's Villa, near Rome.

Sir William Hamilton, a Scottish diplomat who was interested in Roman antiquities, found them in 1770 after draining the lake. The vase is enormous – almost three metres in height – and is made of marble. It was the first item on Napoleon's list of treasures that he wanted to take back to France after conquering Britain. As history tells us, he didn't quite succeed!

Mystery object

What do you think this object was used for?

Answer on page 40

Pearly king

The Emperor Julius Caesar was a keen collector of pearls. It was said that he would sometimes weigh them in the palm of his hand to judge their value. He knew that pearls from Britain were highly valued and of good quality.

Theatre of the north

An enthusiastic amateur archaeologist may have discovered the most northerly amphitheatre in the Roman Empire. It was at the Trimontium fort at Newstead, near Melrose. This theatre may have attracted crowds of over 3000 to watch all kinds of Roman entertainment – such as bear-baiting, executions and military parades.

Signalmen

The Romans were known to be excellent land-surveyors. A series of watch-towers (above) across Tayside was set up to monitor the movements of local people. There would have been a signalling system with beacon fires or smoke between watch-towers and the nearest fort.

The watch-tower at Fendoch looks over the Sma' Glen and north towards the mountains of the Highlands. The Roman legions had to be always prepared for trouble brewing from the folk up north!

On a Roman Helmet

A poem by Will H. Ogilvie (1869–1963)

Ogilvie was a Borderer who lived near Selkirk for many years. His poetry was widely known in his own day, and he had the nickname of 'the Border Kipling'. He has a memorial cairn on the hill road from Selkirk to Roberton. From nearby, you can see the Eildon hilltops, the Roman Trimontium.

A helmet of the legion, this,
　　That long and deep hath lain,
Come back to taste the living kiss
　　Of sun and wind again.
Ah! touch it with a reverent hand,
　　For in its burnished dome
Lies here within this distant land
　　The glory that was Rome!

The tides of sixteen hundred years
　　Have flowed, and ebbed, and flowed,
And yet – I see the tossing spears
　　Come up the Roman Road;
While, high above the trumpets pealed,
　　The eagles lift and fall,
And, all unseen, the War God's shield
　　Floats, guardian, over all!

Who marched beneath this gilded helm?
　　Who wore this casque a-shine?
A leader mighty in the realm?
　　A soldier of the line?
The proud patrician takes his rest
　　The spearman's bones beside,
And earth who knows their secret best
　　Gives this of all their pride!

With sunlight on this golden crest
　　Maybe some Roman guard,
Set free from duty, wandered west
　　Through Memory's gate unbarred;
Or climbing Eildon cleft in three,
　　Grown sick at heart for home,
Looked eastward to the grey North Sea
　　That paved the road to Rome.

Or by the queen of Border streams
　　That flowed his camp beneath
Long dallied with the dearer dreams
　　Of love as old as death,
And doffed this helm to dry lips' need,
　　And dipped it in the tide,
And pledged in brimming wine of Tweed
　　Some maid on Tiber-side.

Years pass; and Time keeps tally,
　　And pride takes earth for tomb,
And down the Melrose valley
　　Corn grows and roses bloom;
The red suns set, the red suns rise,
　　The ploughs lift through the loam,
And in one earth-worn helmet lies
　　The majesty of Rome.

TIMELINE

54 and 55 BC	**Julius Caesar** invades southern Britain from the Roman province of Gallia (France), but doesn't stay.
0	Birth of **Jesus Christ** in Bethlehem in Judea, part of the Roman Empire.
AD 43	Invasion of Britannia by the **Emperor Claudius**.
AD 60–61	A revolt against the Roman occupation in the south of Britannia is led by **Boudicca**.
AD 79–83	**Agricola**, the Roman Governor of Britannia, invades the northern territories, now known as Scotland. The Romans call it **'Caledonia'**.
circa **AD 84**	Battle of Mons Graupius, between the Romans and the Caledonians. The Romans win – many Caledonians are killed.
AD 122	Building of Hadrian's Wall across the north of England, from Wallsend to the Solway Firth.
AD 142–165	**Emperor Antoninus Pius** occupies southern Scotland.
AD 142	The Antonine Wall is built across Scotland from Forth to Clyde. It was given up around AD 163, when the Romans withdrew to Hadrian's Wall.
AD 208–211	**Emperor Severus**, commands his armies in person in Britannia.
AD 400	Hadrian's Wall is abandoned by the Roman army.
AD 410	End of Roman rule in Britain.

ANSWERS

Page 19: **The Bridgeness slab** – The animals visible on the right-hand panel of the slab are a pig (**sus**), a sheep (**ovis**) and a bull (**taurus**).

Page 22: **Health, Roman style** – These medical and surgical instruments are as follows: I = **ligula**, used perhaps as an earpick or a tongue depressor; II = **forceps**, used for gripping firmly on a part of the body; III = **artery forceps**, used for holding firmly on a artery, perhaps to stem blood flow; IV = **spatula**, used for stirring medicines or spreading them on the affected part: V = **cauteries**, four examples of instruments used for searing tissue to stop bleeding or prevent infection.

Page 23: **Rod of Asclepius** – Other organisations that use the symbol of the snake entwined around a staff include NHS ambulance services, the British Medical Association, the Royal Army Medical Corps and the World Health Organisation. The snake can be spotted at the bottom of the right-hand side of the statue.

Page 27: **Number riddles** – A Roman number that becomes one more when one (**I**) is taken away from it is **IX** (9), or **XIX** (19), etc.

A Roman number that becomes ten more when ten is taken away from it is **XL** (40), or **XC** (90), etc.

XVI = 16; **CCV** = 205; **XLII** = 42; **DCIX** = 609; **MD** = 1500; **MMX** = 2010; **DXXX** = 530

Page 29: **Secret message** – 'WINTER ENDLESS IN CALEDONIA. SEND MORE SUPPLIES.'

Page 34: **Typefaces** – A Roman typeface is an up-and-down typeface, whereas an italic typeface is usually *slanted*.

Page 35: **Planets** – Jupiter, Mars, Mercury, Neptune, Pluto*, Saturn, Uranus and Venus. (*Although reclassified as a dwarf planet in 2006 and a plutoid in 2008, Pluto is still considered to be a planet by many people.)

Page 37: **Mystery object** – This is a hat made from hair moss, woven like a basket, from the site at Newstead.

ANSWERS – Facts and activities section

Page ii: **Word search** – Answers in right-hand column.

Page iii: **Gods and goddesses quiz** – A = VII; B = XII; C = XI; D = I; E = VIII; F = II; G = III; H = X; I = IV; J = IX; K = VI; L = V

Page v: **Criss-crossword** – **across:** 4 = optio; 6 = principia; 7 = numerals; **down:** 1 = Caledonia; 2 = Agricola; 4 = onager; 5 = carnyx; 8 = abacus; 9 = strigil

Members of the Ermine Street Guard, a modern-day organisation that researches the Roman army, makes replica weapons and stages re-enactment events.

See the Facts and activities section, page vii, for Places of Interest, including related websites.

The Romans in Scotland
Facts and activities

This book belongs to:

_____

Write your name on the above line.

Word search

Find the following names, objects and phrases from the days of the Romans in the word search below. You can move diagonally, as well as up and down, or straight across, in any direction, to find the listed words.

Answers on page 40

ANTONINE
BATH HOUSE
BRIDGENESS
BRIGANTIA
CENTURION
EMPEROR
FORT
GLADIUS

HADRIAN'S WALL
LEGIONARY
MERCURY
MONS GRAUPIUS
NEWSTEAD
NUMERALS
STRIGIL
VICE VERSA

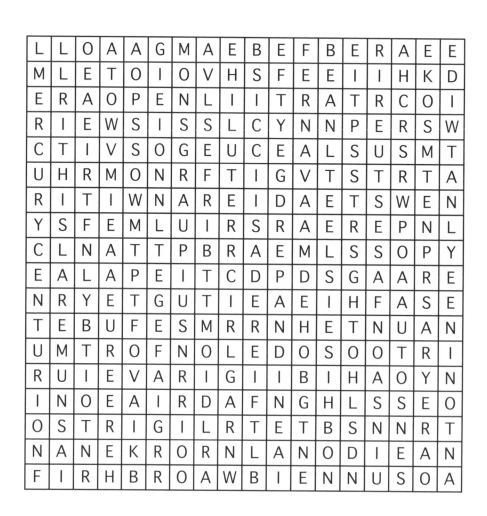

L	L	O	A	A	G	M	A	E	B	E	F	B	E	R	A	E	E
M	L	E	T	O	I	O	V	H	S	F	E	E	I	I	H	K	D
E	R	A	O	P	E	N	L	I	I	T	R	A	T	R	C	O	I
R	I	E	W	S	I	S	S	L	C	Y	N	N	P	E	R	S	W
C	T	I	V	S	O	G	E	U	C	E	A	L	S	U	S	M	T
U	H	R	M	O	N	R	F	T	I	G	V	T	S	T	R	T	A
R	I	T	I	W	N	A	R	E	I	D	A	E	T	S	W	E	N
Y	S	F	E	M	L	U	I	R	S	R	A	E	R	E	P	N	L
C	L	N	A	T	T	P	B	R	A	E	M	L	S	S	O	P	Y
E	A	L	A	P	E	I	T	C	D	P	D	S	G	A	A	R	E
N	R	Y	E	T	G	U	T	I	E	A	E	I	H	F	A	S	E
T	E	B	U	F	E	S	M	R	R	N	H	E	T	N	U	A	N
U	M	T	R	O	F	N	O	L	E	D	O	S	O	O	T	R	I
R	U	I	E	V	A	R	I	G	I	I	B	I	H	A	O	Y	N
I	N	O	E	A	I	R	D	A	F	N	G	H	L	S	S	E	O
O	S	T	R	I	G	I	L	R	T	E	T	B	S	N	N	R	T
N	A	N	E	K	R	O	R	N	L	A	N	O	D	I	E	A	N
F	I	R	H	B	R	O	A	W	B	I	E	N	N	U	S	O	A

Gods and goddesses

Everything in the Roman world had a god or goddess in charge. Match the names of the gods and goddesses to the aspect of Roman life associated with them. (Some are mentioned in this book.)

Answers on page 40

Diana, Minerva, Juno, Vesta and Apollo

A: Bacchus _____

B: Diana _____

C: Janus _____

D: Jupiter _____

E: Mars _____

F: Venus _____

G: Minerva _____

H: Mercury _____

I: Neptune _____

J: Juno _____

K: Vesta _____

L: Apollo _____

I Master of all Roman gods

II Goddess of love and beauty

III Goddess of wisdom, learning and industry

IV Powerful god of the sea

V God of sun, music and light

VI Goddess of hearth and home

VII God of wine and partying

VIII God of war

IX Goddess of women and fertility

X Messenger of the gods

XI God of beginnings and endings

XII Goddess of the moon and hunting

Ludus Caledonia

A game for 2–4 players. Use different coloured counters or buttons or coins for each player. Each throws the dice. The highest scorer wins. Start at **Trimontium** and race your opponents around Caledonia. Avoid the hazards if you can!

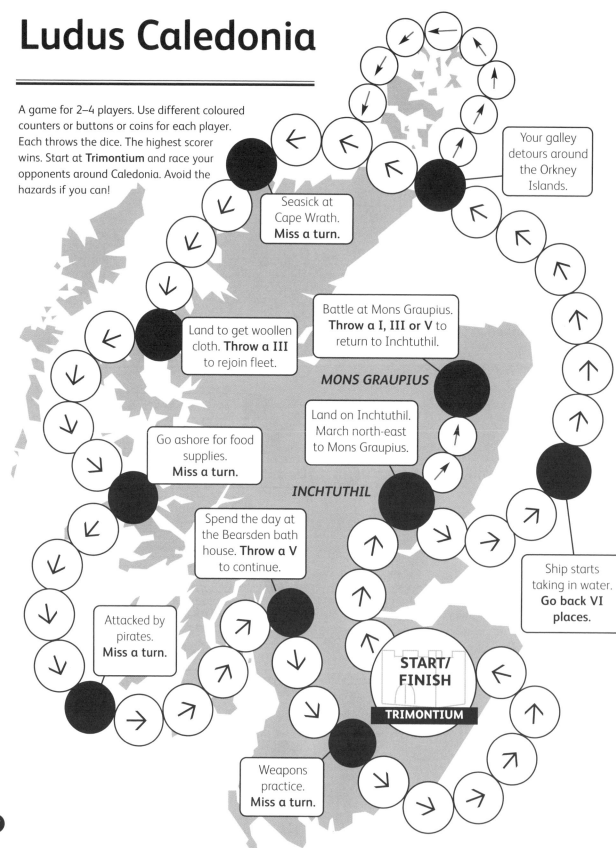

Your galley detours around the Orkney Islands.

Seasick at Cape Wrath. **Miss a turn.**

Battle at Mons Graupius. **Throw a I, III or V to** return to Inchtuthil.

MONS GRAUPIUS

Land to get woollen cloth. **Throw a III** to rejoin fleet.

Land on Inchtuthil. March north-east to Mons Graupius.

INCHTUTHIL

Go ashore for food supplies. **Miss a turn.**

Spend the day at the Bearsden bath house. **Throw a V** to continue.

Ship starts taking in water. **Go back VI places.**

Attacked by pirates. **Miss a turn.**

START/ FINISH

TRIMONTIUM

Weapons practice. **Miss a turn.**

Criss-crossword

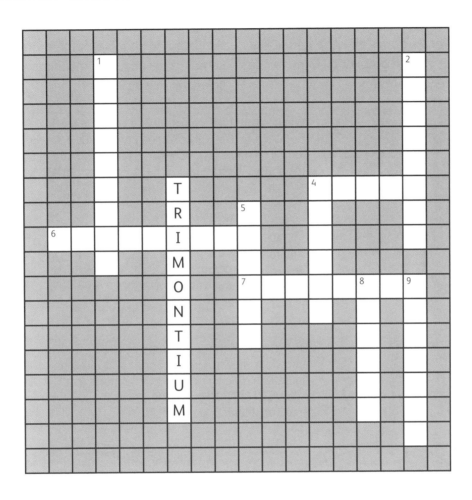

Answer the following questions to complete this word puzzle.

(Answers on page 40)

Across

4. A Roman soldier, second in command to the centurion. (See page 7)
6. The HQ within a Roman fort. (See p. 11)
7. Clocks and watches often have Roman _____ on them. (See page 35)

Down

1. The Roman name for Scotland. (See p. 4)
2. Roman general who invaded Scotland in around AD 79. (See page 3)
4. Catapult that fired huge stones over 200 metres. (See page 31)
5. Celtic war trumpet. (See page 9)
8. Some merchants used an _____ for quicker calculations. (See page 27)
9. Bath-house scraper. (See page 24)

Design a coin

The Romans struck coins to commemorate new emperors, victories in battle and also to symbolise gods and goddesses. Many made direct reference to affairs in Britain.

Design a new coin to celebrate something significant in your life. Some examples of Roman coins and their meanings are shown below for inspiration.

When Vespasian became the Emperor of Rome, it was seen as a fresh start for the whole Roman Empire. The emperor is seen raising a female (who represents Rome) from the ground, while the god Minerva looks on. The motto reads 'ROMA RESURGES' – 'Rome, thou shalt rise again'.

On the front of the coin is the Emperor Commodus, and on the reverse is Britannia seated on a rock. Britannia has a standard in her right hand – a symbol of a garrisoned (occupied by troops) province. The spear in her left hand and the shield resting on a helmet signify her strength and warlike spirit.

On the front of the coin is Hadrian, and on the reverse the emperor is shown in priestly robes; opposite him is a female figure with a victim at her feet. The motto reads 'ADVENTVS AVG[VSTI] BRITANNIÆ' – the arrival of Augustus [the emperor] in Britain.

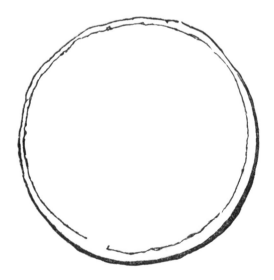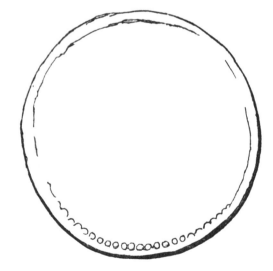

FRONT

REVERSE

PLACES OF INTEREST

Listed below are a number of places associated with the Romans. For additional information, contact local Tourist Information offices.

Annan Museum, **Annan**. Romans established large camps and fortifications in Annandale.

www.annan.org.uk

Moat Park Heritage Centre, **Biggar**. Displays on the Romans in Clydesdale.

www.biggarmuseumtrust.co.uk

Kinneil Museum, **Bo'ness**. Kinneil Roman fortlet.

www.falkirkcommunitytrust.org/ venues/kinneil-museum

Dumfries Museum, **Dumfries**. Finds from the Birrens and collections of carved stones.

www.dumfriesmuseum.demon.co.uk

McManus Galleries, **Dundee**. Material from the legionary fortress at Carpow, near Newburgh, on the south bank of the Firth of Tay.

www.dundeecity.gov.uk

Cramond, **Edinburgh**. The fort on the river (*Caer Amon*) which guarded the eastern flank and supply station for the Antonine Wall.

National Museum of Scotland, **Edinburgh**. Find lots of information and many objects featured in this book including coins, weapons, the Bridgeness slab, Cramond Lioness and the Deskford Carnyx.

www.nms.ac.uk/scotland

Rough Castle, near **Falkirk**. One of the best preserved of the 19 forts on the Antonine Wall.

Bearsden Bath-house, **Glasgow**. Close to the well-preserved remains of a 2nd-century fort.

www.historic-scotland.gov.uk

Hunterian Museum, **Glasgow**. Display of distance slabs from the Antonine Wall.

www.hunterian.gla.ac.uk

Kelvingrove Museum, **Glasgow**. Examples of Roman finds in the west of Scotland.

www.glasgowlife.org.uk/museums

Auld Kirk Museum, **Kirkintilloch**. Finds from Bar Hill.

www.eastdunbarton.gov.uk

Melrose Abbey Museum, **Melrose**. Finds from the site at Newstead.

www.historic-scotland.gov.uk

The Trimontium Trust, **Melrose**. Become a Trimontium trooper of the new Twentieth Legion at the Fort of the Three Hills.

www.trimontium.org.uk

Perth Museum & Art Gallery, **Perth**. Look for the inscribed stone from the fort at Bertha.

www.pkc.gov.uk

ROMAN ROADS IN SCOTLAND

There may be Roman roads near where you live. Check the website **www.heritagepaths.co.uk** – It gives maps and details of walks along the routes of old Roman roads.

Borders

– **Dere Street** was the main Roman road into Scotland, which ran from Durham to the Firth of Forth.

Strathclyde and Lanarkshire

– **Military Way**, from Twechar to Castlecary, was part of the Antonine Wall and used by Roman patrols on the south side of the Wall.

Dumfries and Galloway

– **Elvanfoot Roman Road** is another ancient route going from the River Nith at Drumlanrig, through the Dalveen Pass, to Elvanfoot in the Clyde valley.

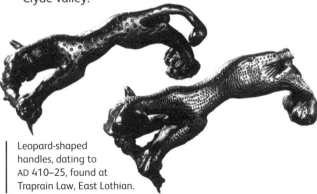

Leopard-shaped handles, dating to AD 410–25, found at Traprain Law, East Lothian.

Stories about Romans in Britain

Theresa Breslin – *Across the Roman Wall* (1997)
Peter Connolly
    The Roman Army (1975)
    The Cavalryman (1988)
    The Legionary (1988)
    The Roman Fort (1991)
Frances Hendry
    Victoria: Born to be a Fighter! (2004)
Mollie Hunter – *The Stronghold* (1974)
Mick Manning – *Roman Fort* (2006)

K. M. Peyton – *Minna's Quest* (2007)
Rosemary Sutcliff
    The Eagle of the Ninth (1954)
    Outcast (1955)
    The Silver Branch (1957)
    The Lantern Bearers (1959)
    Song for a Dark Queen (1978)
    Eagles Honour (1995)
    Frontier Wolf (2008)
Henry Treece
    Legions of the Eagle (1954)

FURTHER CREDITS

THE COMPREHENSIVE HISTORY OF ENGLAND: Civil, Military, Religious, Intellectual and Social – Macfarlane and Thomson (Blackie & Son, Glasgow, n.d.) – for pages 4 (Caledonians); 13 (war galley); 14 (Hadrian); 15 (Hadrian's Wall map); 18 (Antonine Wall map, adapted); 29 (Julius Caesar)
THE ROMAN WALL – Rev. J Collingwood Bruce (Longman, Green, Reader and Dyer, Newcastle-upon-Tyne, 1807) – for pages 14 (background of wall, stone marker), 18 (distance slab); Facts and activities section – page iii (gods and goddesses; vi (coins)
AUTHOR'S COLLECTION, out of copyright. Licensor www.scran.ac.uk – for page 23 (Trajan's column, scene)
© CITY OF EDINBURGH COUNCIL/NATIONAL MUSEUMS SCOTLAND – for page 12 (Cramond Lioness)
HISTORIC SCOTLAND © Crown copyright reproduced courtesy of Historic Scotland. www.historicscotlandimages.gov.uk – page 24 (Bearsden bath-house); 37 (Roman watch-tower reconstruction)
NATIONAL MUSEUMS SCOTLAND (cont'd) – for pages 19 (Bridgeness slab); 20 (reconstruction of Roman cooking utensils); 21 (quern, *mortarium*, pot); 22 (surgical instruments from Cramond fort); 25 (dies, counters); 27 (abacus, calculator); 28 (stylus, Bridgeness slab detail); 29 (stylus, writing tablet); 30 (sword, background Eildon Hills); 30–31 (wheel); 31 (key, shoe, leather, javelin heads, calthrops); 32 (Roman hoard, Falkirk Tartan and diagram, seascape); 33 (amphora, seascape); 34 (viaduct at Leaderfoot); 35 (sundial); 36 (Roman nail); 37 (Roman hat); 40 (Ermine Street Guard); Facts and activities section – page vii (leopard-shaped handles)
© NEWSQUEST (HERALD AND TIMES). Licensor www.scran.ac.uk – for page 36 (Warwick vase)
© MATTHIAS KABEL, http://commons,wikipedia.org/wiki/File:Groma – for page 27 (*groma*)
© ALAN BRABY – for pages 8–9 (battle scenes and illustration of carnyx); 17 (soldier on duty); Facts and activities section – page i (Romans off-duty)

© FRANCES JARVIE – for pages 5 (crannog); 19 (lillia); 23 (St Bernard's Well, Edinburgh)
© CARRIE PHILIP – for pages 2 (recruitment poster); 6–7 (army ranks); 20 (bread oven); 21 (edible dormouse); 25 (Romans in bath-house)
© CATHERINE J REID – for poem used on page 38, 'On a Roman Helmet', Will H. Ogilvie (1869–1963). Used by kind permission.
© ROSEMARY SUTCLIFF – for extract used on page 14, from her novel *Frontier Wolf* (2008). Used by kind permission.

OTHER TITLES IN THE SCOTTIES SERIES (eds Frances and Gordon Jarvie)

The Clans (Gordon Jarvie)
The Covenanters (Claire Watts)
Flight in Scotland (Frances and Gordon Jarvie)
Greyfriars Bobby: A Tale of Victorian Edinburgh (Frances and Gordon Jarvie)
The Jacobites (Antony Kamm)
Mary, Queen of Scots (Elizabeth Douglas)
Robert Burns in Time and Place (Frances and Gordon Jarvie)
Scotland's Vikings (Frances and Gordon Jarvie)
Scottish Rocks and Fossils (Alan and Moira McKirdy)
Scottish Kings and Queens (Elizabeth Douglas)
Supernatural Scotland (Eileen Dunlop)

Visit National Museums Scotland's Learning and Programmes teachers' resources at
www.nms.ac.uk/education/schools/teachers_resources/downloads.aspx
for more fun facts and help to get the most out of your visit to the
National Museum of Scotland in Edinburgh.